BACH CANTATAS REQUIRING LIMITED RESOURCES

A Guide to Editions

William J. Bullock

UNIVERSITY
PRESS OF
AMERICA

LANHAM • NEW YORK • LONDON

Library of Congress Cataloging in Publication Data

Bullock, William J.
  Bach cantatas requiring limited resources.

  1. Bach, Johann Sebastian, 1685–1750 –
Bibliography. 2. Bach, Johann Sebastian, 1685–1750.
Cantatas. I. Title.
ML134.B1B9   1984   016.7828'2'0924   84–2337
ISBN 0–8191–3863–0 (alk. paper)

To my wife,
Janie Lee

CONTENTS

PART 4 / APPENDICES

PREFACE

Several years ago when I began conducting a community chorus on a regular basis, I embarked on a continuing search for so-called "major works" that could be performed by a reasonably accomplished though relatively small chorus, and that would not require expenditure of an excessively large portion of an already meager budget for instrumentalists. I soon discovered, as many others have, a wealth of material among the 200-plus cantatas of J. S. Bach. Of course, isolating the specific cantatas that met my needs was a considerable task, and locating performance material was frustrating at best.

With the tricentennial of Bach's birth approaching, it occurred to me that others might make good use of the information I had assembled. So I have attempted to put it into a usable format, knowing full well that imperfections are bound to manifest themselves. I hope, though, that they have been kept to a minimum.

I am pleased to express my gratitude to the publishers listed herein, who assisted me in assembling the publication information on specific editions, and to my wife and children, who understandingly accepted my absence from family activities while I was assembling, arranging, and setting down the information in this guide. The final stages of my research were partially supported by a Faculty Development Grant from Columbus College. The support of my colleagues and College is greatly appreciated.

I have made a determined effort to assure that the details in the catalog of cantatas are accurate. For any errors that may remain, whether they be due to erroneous information supplied to me by others or misunderstandings or oversights on my own behalf, I apologize to the reader, who I hope, nonetheless, will find this a useful, timesaving reference.

Columbus, Georgia   WILLIAM J. BULLOCK
November 1983

vii

PART 1 / ABBREVIATIONS AND ADDRESSES

ABBREVIATIONS FOR LANGUAGES, VOICINGS, AND GENERAL TERMS

A	choral altos
a	alto solo
arr	arranger(s)
B	choral basses
b	bass solo
ch/pts	individual choral parts
ch/s	full choral score
ed, eds	edition or editor, editions
Eng	English
Fr	French
f/s	full score
Ger	German
inst	instrument(s)
inst/pts	instrumental parts
min	minute(s)
m/s	miniature score
no.	number
p, pp	page, pages
pv/s	piano-vocal score
S	choral sopranos
s	soprano solo
T	choral tenors
t	tenor solo
vol., vols.	volume, volumes
( )	denotes *alternative* instrument or voice
[ ]	denotes *optional* instrument or voice

ABBREVIATIONS FOR INSTRUMENTS

bn	bassoon(s)
brh	baritone horn(s)
cto	continuo
eh	English horn(s)
eup	euphonium(s)
fl	flute(s)
hn	horn(s)
kbd	keyboard
ob	oboe(s)
ob da caccia	oboe(s) da caccia
ob d'amore	oboe(s) d'amore
org	organ
rc	recorder(s)
str	strings
tba	tuba(s)
trb	trombone(s)
trp	trumpet(s)
va	viola(s)
va da gamba	viola(s) da gamba
vc	violoncello(s)
vn	violin(s)
ww	woodwinds

ABBREVIATIONS FOR STUDY SCORE SOURCES

BBL   Broude Brothers Limited Miniature Score (see Publishers' Addresses)

BG   J. S. Bach: *Werke,* ed. Bach-Gesellschaft, Leipzig (Leipzig: Breitkopf & Härtel, 1851-99, reprinted, 1947)

BV   Bärenreiter-Verlag Taschenpartitur (see Publishers' Addresses)

CM   *Choral Music,* ed. Ray Robinson (New York: W. W. Norton & Co., 1978)

DCS   *Dessoff Choir Series,* ed. Paul Boepple (New York: Music Press, Inc., 1941-48)

EE   Ernst Eulenberg Pocket Score (see Publishers' Addresses)

EGC   *Eleven Great Cantatas,* reprinted from *BG* (New York: Dover Publications, Inc., 1976)

Kalmus   Edwin F. Kalmus Miniature Score (see Publishers' Addresses)

Lea   Lea Pocket Score (see Publishers' Addresses)

NAsW   J. S. Bach: *Neue Ausgabe sämtlicher Werke,* ed. Johann-Sebastian-Bach-Institut, Göttingen, and the Bach-Archiv, Leipzig (Kassel and Basle: Bärenreiter, 1954-)

NBG   J. S. Bach: *Veröffentlichungen der neuen Bachgesellschaft,* ed. Neue Bachgesellschaft, Leipzig (Leipzig: Breitkopf & Härtel, 1901-)

Ph   Philharmonia Pocket Score (see Publishers' Addresses)

ABBREVIATIONS AND ADDRESSES OF PUBLISHERS, DOMESTIC AGENTS, AND PARENT COMPANIES

AB	Alexander Broude, Inc., 225 West 57th Street, New York, NY 10019
AMP	Associated Music Publishers, Inc., 866 Third Avenue, New York, NY 10022
BBL	Broude Brothers Limited, 170 Varick Street, New York, NY 10013
BMP	Belwin Mills Publishing Corporation, Melville, NY 11746
Bo&H	Boosey & Hawkes, Inc., 200 Smith Street, Farmingdale, NY 11735
Br&H-L	VEB Breitkopf & Härtel Musikverlag, Postschliessfach 147, DDR-701 Leipzig, East Germany (Agent: AB)
Br&H-W	Breitkopf & Härtel Musikverlag, Postfach 1707, D-6200 Wiesbaden 1, West Germany (Agent: AMP)
BV	Bärenreiter-Verlag, Postfact 10 03 29, 3500 Kassel, West Germany (Agents: EAM and M-B)
CF	Carl Fischer, Inc., 62 Cooper Square, New York, NY 10003
CFP	C. F. Peters Corporation, 373 Park Avenue South, New York, NY 10016
Choudens	Maison Choudens, 38 Rue Jean Mermoz, Paris 8, France (Agent: CFP)
Con	Concordia Publishing House, 3558 South Jefferson Avenue, St. Louis, MO 63118
Curwen	J. Curwen & Sons, 140 Strand, London WC2R 1HH, England (Agent: GS)
EAM	European American Music Distributors Corporation, 11 West End Road, Totowa, NJ 07512
EBM	Edward B. Marks Music Corporation (Parent Company: BMP)
ECS	E. C. Schirmer Music Company, 112 South Street, Boston, MA 02111
EE	Ernst Eulenburg Ltd., 48 Great Marlborough Street, London W1V 1DB, England (Agent: EAM)
Galaxy	Galaxy Music Corporation, 131 West 86th Street, Ninth Floor, New York, NY 10024
GS	G. Schirmer, Inc., 866 Third Avenue, New York, NY 10022
HV	Hänssler-Verlag, Postfach 1220, D 7303 Neuhausen-Stuttgart, West Germany (Agent: MFM)
HWG	H. W. Gray Company (Parent Company: BMP)
Kalmus	Edwin F. Kalmus & Company, Inc., P. O. Box 1007, Opa-Locka, FL 33054 (Agent for piano-vocal scores only: BMP)

Lea	Lea Pocket Scores (Agent: EAM)
M-B	Magnamusic-Baton, Inc., 10370 Page Industrial Blvd., St. Louis, MO 63132
MFM	Mark Foster Music Company, Box 4012, Champaign, IL 61820
Novello	Novello and Company, Ltd., 8 Lower James Street, London W1R 4DN, England
OUP	Oxford University Press, Music Department, 200 Madison Avenue, New York, NY 10016
Ph	Philharmonia Pocket Scores (Agent: EAM)
TP	Theodore Presser Company, Presser Place, Bryn Mawr, PA 19010

PART 2 / INTRODUCTION

BACKGROUND

In recent years the cantatas of J. S. Bach have received performances with increasing frequency. Yet, except for a few of the more widely known ones, they remain relatively unexplored by performers with limited resources or little expertise. Three reasons for this neglect may be discerned: the staggering number of the cantatas as a whole (over 200), the necessity of assembling an orchestra to perform them, and the difficulty of locating performance material suitable to the specific needs of a particular performing group.

This guide addresses these reasons for neglect in an effort to promote more frequent and wider spread performances of Bach's cantatas. Since the groups most likely to organize these performances are independent choral societies, church choirs, and college choral ensembles, the reasons for neglect are approached from the perspective of a choral organization. The result is a catalog of those cantatas (numbering 47 in all, a more manageable figure) that are most likely to be performable by choral organizations of limited means.

More and more, performers at all levels of expertise are demanding that Baroque music be performed in a stylistically accurate manner. Although questions of performance practice are not the subject of this guide, [1] something must be said about the propriety of a smaller choral group undertaking the performance of a Bach cantata. If the use of a small choral group could ever be considered improper, such is not the case with the cantatas cataloged here. The second criterion used in selecting the cantatas to be cataloged (see below) has precluded that possibility. In fact, the chance of a clean, buoyant performance, as befits the style of the period, will be improved when the choral and instrumental forces used are not unduly large.

CRITERIA USED TO SELECT THE CANTATAS CATALOGED

The two criteria applied in selection of the cantatas cataloged are based on the assumption that choral organizations of limited means would usually seek to perform cantatas that include a considerable amount of choral writing but require as small an orchestra as is artistically feasible. The first criterion, then,

---

[1] A practical and cogent book on the subject, also addressed to the layman, is Paul Steinitz's *Performing Bach's Vocal Music* (Croydon, England: Addington Press, 1980, licensed in the USA to Hinshaw Music, Inc.)

stipulated that no cantata would be included that did not include at least one choral number other than the customary concluding chorale. The second criterion provided that no cantata would be included that required more instruments than a string ensemble plus two woodwind instruments, unless the additional instruments merely double other instruments or voices. By excluding cantatas with fuller scorings and those with brass instruments that function independently, as opposed to doubling a cantus firmus or other part, the resulting catalog consists of those cantatas that groups with limited forces might most easily produce without sacrificing appropriate balance among the parts.

CONSIDERATIONS REGARDING ALTERNATIVE INSTRUMENTATION, SOLO VOICING, AND LANGUAGE

When circumstances are particularly restrictive, performance of a cantata may be possible only if doubling instruments are omitted and/or certain solo parts assigned to the appropriate choral section. Although the distinctive colors of Bach's scoring would be compromised, the alternative of no performance at all is certainly less desirable.[2] Accordingly, the annotation of each entry in the catalog includes a reference to any instruments lacking a distinct part in certain or all movements of the cantata. Similarly, those solos or vocal ensembles whose ornamentation and melodic leaps are sufficiently limited to permit performance by a choral section (e.g., chorale melodies) are identified. If any particular solo voice is thereby rendered optional so far as the whole cantata is concerned, this fact is reflected in the line of the entry that lists the cantata's scoring. (See Appendix II for a list of cantatas performable with various solo voices.)

Another consideration raised by Bach's scoring of the cantatas is the desirability of substituting modern instruments for unusual or obsolete ones. Professional organizations, not to mention amateur ones, have difficulty locating performers for certain instruments scored by Bach in many of his cantatas. It is entirely reasonable, therefore, to substitute an appropriate modern instrument for these older ones, though this may make it necessary to copy out a new part. In the catalog, suggested alternative instruments are given in the line of each entry that lists the cantata's scoring. This is true for all older instruments except the oboe d'amore. When performing a cantata requiring one or more oboes d'amore, it will be necessary to study the score to

---

[2]W. Gilles Whittaker suggests various alternative performing forces for all the cantatas (by omitting doubling instruments, replacing obsolete instruments, and/or replacing woodwinds with strings) in the appendices of his *Fugitive Notes on Certain Cantatas and the Motets of J. S. Bach* (London: Oxford University Press, 1924).

discover whether or not the range of each part in question permits substitution of an oboe or an English horn. If not, three other alternatives exist: both an oboe and an English horn might be used, if the part is edited carefully; problematical phrases or portions thereof might be transposed; or authenticity might be totally ignored and a clarinet substituted.

Newer editions of the cantatas sometimes include parts for alternative instruments. They are also less likely than older ones to be marred by nineteenth-century editorial accretions, and more likely to include an accurate realization of the continuo part.

Selection of appropriate instruments for realization of Bach's continuo parts is critical to an effective performance. Of course, the fundamental requirement is that the part be realized by keyboard and bass instruments. In the case of the cantatas cataloged here, the appropriate choice of keyboard instrument is the organ. A harpsichord might be substituted if necessary, and although substitution of a piano would completely undermine authenticity, even this is preferable to leaving Bach's music on the library shelf. Generally, the practical choice of bass instrument(s) is one or more cellos and double basses, depending on the size of the total instrumental ensemble. It is often wise to include a bassoon as well, especially when treble woodwinds are present. An expedient in pressing circumstances might be elimination of the bassoon and even of the double bass, though in the latter instance the absence of the lower octave would be sorely missed. The catalog lists the continuo designation only if it is specifically scored (e.g., cto-org, cto-bn).

Regarding the language of the text in various editions, it goes without saying that only the German is original and translations vary in quality. Some translations seem awkward or affected, but a more serious problem of many is their failure to retain the composer's associations between certain crucial words and particular musical gestures. When it is impractical to perform a cantata in German and when more than one translation is available, every effort should be made to compare the translations and to select for performance the edition with the more faithful translation.

FORMAT AND CONTENT OF THE CATALOG ENTRIES

This catalog of cantatas is intended to assist prospective performers in locating works whose outward characteristics make them candidates for further consideration. (See Appendix III for a list of the works by occasional appropriateness.) Detailed descriptions of the cantatas are not provided, for this information is available elsewhere.[3] Of course, the music itself should be

---

[3]See, for example, W. Gilles Whittaker, *The Cantatas of Johann Sebastian Bach, Sacred and Secular,* 2 paperback vols.

consulted, by referring to the study scores listed or to other sources, before making the final selection of a cantata to perform. Entries are made in numerical order according to the *Bachgesellschaft (BG)* numbering of the cantatas. After each cantata's number, the following information is given in the order indicated:

1. German title with an English translation in parentheses
2. Date of composition[4]
3. Occasion for which the cantata was composed[5]
4. Number of pages of the *BG* edition
5. Approximate duration[6]

Choral, solo, and instrumental scorings are given next. This information is emphasized by setting it flush against the left margin. Slash marks separate the scorings, the choral scoring being given first (in upper case Roman type), the solo scoring second (in lower case italic type), and the instrumental scoring last (in lower case Roman type). Parentheses denote alternative scorings; brackets indicate optional scorings.

Following the information on scoring, recently or currently available editions are enumerated. The editions are entered one to a line in no particular order, except that those available for purchase and/or those including an English translation precede those that are available only on a rental basis or those that do

---

(London: Oxford University Press, 1978 re-issue of the 1959 edition); Philipp Spitta, *Johann Sebastian Bach, His Work and Influence on the Music of Germany,* trans. Clara Bell and J. A. Fuller-Maitland, 3 vols. (New York: Dover Publications, 1951 re-issue of the 1885 edition); Werner Neumann, *Handbuch der Kantaten Joh. Seb. Bachs,* 2nd ed. (Leipzig: Breitkopf & Härtel, 1953); Fredrich Smend, *Johann Sebastian Bach: Kirchen-Kantaten,* 3rd ed. (Berlin: Christlicher Zeitschriftenverlag, 1966); and the references cited in notes 1, 2, 4, and 5.

[4]As arrived at in the recent research of Alfred Dürr and published in his *Die Kantaten von Johann Sebastian Bach* (Kassel: Bärenreiter Verlag, 1971) and *Zur Chronologie der Leipziger Vokalwerke J. S. Bachs* (Kassel: Bärenreiter Verlag, 1976).

[5]As given by Charles Sanford Terry in *Joh. Seb. Bach Cantata Texts, Sacred and Secular* (London: The Holland Press, 1964).

[6]As listed in David Daniels, *Orchestral Music: A Source Book* (Metuchen, N.J.: The Scarecrow Press, Inc., 1972), pp. 7-23.

not include an English translation. Data about each edition are given as follows:

1. In parentheses: editor, if known; an abbreviation for the publisher; publisher's number, for the full score unless followed by the notation "pv/s" (for piano-vocal score); copyright date, if known.
2. After the parentheses: an abbreviation indicating the language(s) of the text underlayed to the music; statements concerning types of performance material available and terms for acquiring it.

If no statement about availability of performance material or terms of acquisition is given, one may generally assume that the edition in question is currently in print, that all performance material is available for sale, and that the choral part is available only in a piano-vocal score. Exceptions to this general rule are stated. Specifically, out-of-print editions are identified, performance material that is unavailable or only available on rental is indicated (if *all* material must be rented, the statement "material on rental" is made), and the availability either of a full choral score (ch/s) or of individual choral parts (ch/pts) is noted.

Each entry continues with an annotation. In general it consists of a listing, in order, of the formal type and the scoring of each of the cantata's movements (to give some impression of the amount of material alloted to the various voices and instruments), an indication of which instruments, if any, have no distinct part (and thus might be omitted), and identification of those solos or vocal ensembles, if any, which could be effectively performed by choral sections.

Concluding each entry is a list of study scores. Collected editions containing a score of the cantata are cited by an appropriate abbreviation (in italic type). Miniature scores are listed using the abbreviation (in Roman type) for the publisher, together with the publisher's number and the notation "m/s" (for miniature score). Some of the listed volumes of the new collected edition of Bach's works, *Neue Ausgabe sämtlicher Werke (NAsW)*, have not yet been published.

15

PART 3 / A CATALOG OF SELECTED CANTATAS

No. 2, *Ach, Gott, vom Himmel sieh darein (O God, From Heav'n Look Down and See)*, 1724, second Sunday after Trinity, 18pp, 20min.
SATB / *atb* / 2ob, 4trb, 2vn, va, cto

(G. Raphael -- Br&H-L 7002-pv/s) Ger-Eng, rent f/s & inst/pts
(Br&H-W 7002-pv/s) Ger-Eng, no inst/pts
(Kalmus 9313-pv/s) Ger, no inst/pts

Six movements: Chorus (cto, remaining instruments doubling chorus); Recitative (*t*, cto); Aria (*a*, vn solo, cto); Recitative and Arioso (*b*, str, cto); Aria (*t*, str, 2ob doubling vnI); Chorale (tutti doubling chorus). Two oboes and trombones merely double other parts.
Study scores: *BG*, vol. 1; *NAsW*, series 1, vol. 16; Kalmus, no. 805-m/s.

No. 3, *Ach Gott, wie manches Herzeleid (O God, How Grievous Is the Woe)*, 1725, second Sunday after Epiphany, 20pp, 31min.
SATB / *satb* / 2ob d'amore, hn, trb, 2vn, va, cto

(G. Raphael -- Br&H-L 7003-pv/s) Ger-Eng, rent f/s & inst/pts
(E. H. Thorne -- Br&H-W 7003-pv/s, 1958), Ger-Eng, ch/s, no inst/pts
(Kalmus 9314-pv/s) Ger, no inst/pts
(H. Clough-Leighter -- ECS 1613-pv/s, 1931) Ger-Eng, choral movements only

Six movements: Chorus (tutti except for hn); Recitative and Chorale (SATB, *satb*, cto); Aria (*b*, cto); Recitative (*t*, cto); Duet (*sa*, ob d'amore & vn in unison, cto); Chorale (tutti, except trb, doubling chorus). The horn and trombone merely double choral parts.
Study scores: *BG*, vol. 1; *NAsW*, series 1, vol. 5; Kalmus, no. 805-m/s.

No. 4, *Christ lag in Todesbanden (Christ Lay in Death's Dark Prison)*, c. 1708, Easter, 28pp, 24min.
Con ed: TTBB / [*ttbb*] / kbd
Other eds: SATB / [*satb*] / cornetto(trp), 3trb, 2vn, 2va, cto

(Br&H-W 4504, 1965) Ger-Eng, ch/s
(Kalmus 2493) Ger-Eng
(GS 2036-pv/s) Ger-Eng
(John E. West -- Novello 07-0003-0700-pv/s) Ger-Eng, rent inst/pts
(HWG GB-386-pv/s) Eng, rent inst/pts
(G. Schreck -- Br&H-L 7004-pv/s) Ger, rent f/s & inst/pts
(CF RCO-B7) Ger, no ch/s, rent inst/pts
(William B. Heyne, arr -- Con no number-TTBB, 1940) Eng, no inst/pts, out of print

Eight movements: Sinfonia (str, cto); Chorus (tutti); Duet (*sa*, cto); Aria (*t*, unison vn, cto); Chorus (cto); Aria (*b*, str and cto); Duet (*st*, cto); Chorale (tutti doubling chorus). Cornetto and trombone merely double voices in movements 2, 3, and 8. All arias and duets are suitable for performance by choral sections. The Con edition is an arrangement of the composer's original SATB composition.
Study scores: *BG*, vol. 1; *NBG*, Jahrgang 2-2; *NAsW*, series 1, vol. 9; *Bach: Cantata No. 4*, a Norton Critical Score, Gerhard Herz, ed., 1967; Kalmus, no. 805-m/s; *EGC*; EE, no. 1011-m/s; BBL, no. 89-m/s.

No. 7, *Christ unser Herr zum Jordan kam (To Jordan's Stream Came Christ Our Lord)*, 1724, St. John's Day, 32pp, 27min.
SATB / *atb* / 2ob d'amore, 2vn, va, cto

(G. Raphael -- Br&H-L 7007-pv/s) Ger-Eng, rent f/s & inst/pts
(Charles Sanford Terry -- Br&H-W 7007-pv/s, 1930) Ger-Eng, no inst/pts
(Kalmus 4483) Ger

Seven movements: Chorus (tutti plus solo vn); Aria (*b*, cto); Recitative (*t*, cto); Aria (*t*, 2 solo vn, cto); Recitative and Arioso (*b*, str, cto); Aria (*a*, str, cto, 2ob d'amore doubling vnI); Chorale (tutti doubling chorus). The two oboes d'amore have separate parts in the first movement only.
Study scores: *BG*, vol. 1; *NAsW*, series 1, vol. 29; EE, no. 1039-m/s; Kalmus, no. 806-m/s.

No. 9, *Es ist das Heil uns kommen her (Salvation Now Is Come to Earth)*, c. 1732, sixth Sunday after Trinity, 30pp, 27min.
SATB / [sa]tb / fl, ob d'amore, 2vn, va, cto

(Br&H-W 4509) Ger, ch/s
(Br&H-L 7009-pv/s) Ger, rent f/s & inst/pts
(Kalmus 6525) Ger, no inst/pts

Seven movements: Chorus (tutti); Recitative (*b*, cto); Aria (*t*, vn, cto); Recitative and Arioso (*b*, cto); Duet (*sa*, fl, ob d'amore, cto); Recitative (*b*, cto); Chorale (tutti doubling chorus). The flute and oboe d'amore have separate parts in movements 1 and 5. The duet is suitable for performance by the S and A choral sections.
Study scores: *BG*, vol. 1; *NAsW*, series 1, vol. 17; Kalmus, no. 807-m/s.

No. 10, *Meine Seel' erhebt den Herren (My Soul Exhalts the Lord)*, 1724, Visitation of the Blessed Virgin Mary, 27pp, 24min.
SATB / s[a]tb / 2ob, tromba da tirarsi(trp), 2vn, va, cto

(Br&H-W 4510, 1962) Ger-Eng, ch/s
(P. Steinitz -- Curwen 3741-pv/s, 1959) Eng-Ger
(G. Raphael -- Br&H-L 7101-pv/s) Ger, rent f/s & inst/pts
(Kalmus 4489) Ger
(H. Clough-Leighter -- ECS 1614-pv/s, 1931) Ger-Eng, choral movements only

Seven movements: Chorus (tutti); Aria (*s*, 2ob in unison, str, cto); Recitative (*t*, cto); Aria (*b*, cto); Duet (*at*, 2ob and tromba in unison, cto); Recitative (*t*, str, cto); Chorale (tutti doubling chorus). The tromba merely doubles S in the first and last movements and the oboes in the first movement. The *at* duet is suitable for performance by the AT choral sections.
Study scores: *BG*, vol. 1; *NAsW*, series 1, vol. 28; Kalmus, no. 807-m/s.

21

No. 17, *Wer Dank opfert, der preiset mich (Whoso Doth Offer Thanks)*, 1726, fourteenth Sunday after Trinity, 26pp, 22min.
SATB / satb / 2ob, 2vn, va, cto

(Alfred Dürr -- BV no number) Ger, ch/s
(Hans Grischkat -- HV 10.143) Ger-Eng, ch/s
(Br&H-W 4517) Ger, ch/s
(Kalmus 2497) Ger
(Br&H-L 7017-pv/s) Ger, rent f/s & inst/pts
(John E. West -- Novello no number) Eng, material on rental
(W. G. Whittaker -- OUP 46.482-pv/s, 1928) Eng-Ger, rent inst/pts, out of print

    Seven movements in two parts: Part I: Chorus (tutti); Recitative (*a*, cto); Aria (*s*, 2vn, cto). Part II: Recitative (*t*, cto); Aria (*t*, str, cto); Recitative (*b*, cto); Chorale (tutti doubling chorus). The two oboes have separate parts in the first movement only.
    Study scores: *BG*, vol. 2; *NAsW*, series 1, vol. 21; EE, no. 1058-m/s; Kalmus, no. 809-m/s.

No. 22, *Jesus nahm zu sich die Zwölfe (Jesus Called to Him the Twelve)*, 1723, Quinquagesima, 26pp, 20min.
SATB / atb / ob, 2vn, va, cto

(Br&H-W 4522, 1969) Ger, ch/s
(B. Todt -- Br&H-L 7022-pv/s) Ger, rent f/s & inst/pts
(Kalmus 6533-pv/s) Ger, no inst/pts
(OUP no number-pv/s, 1927) Eng, out of print

    Five movements: Arioso and Chorus (SATB, *tb*, all inst); Aria (*a*, ob solo, cto); Recitative (*b*, str, cto); Aria (*t*, str, cto); Chorale (tutti, ob doubling vnI). The oboe has a separate part in the first two movements only. The *a* aria is suitable for performance by the A section.
    Study scores: *BG*, vol. 5; *NAsW*, series 1, vol. 8; Kalmus, no. 810-m/s.

No. 23, *Du wahrer Gott und Davids Sohn (The Very God and David's Son)*, 1723, Quinquagesima, 30pp, 18min.
SATB / [sa]t / 2ob, cornetto(trp), 3trb, 2vn, va, cto

(Hans Grischkat -- HV 10.026, 1966) Ger-Eng, ch/s
(Br&H-W 4523, 1965) Ger-Eng, ch/s
(E. H. Thorne & G. W. Daisley -- Br&H-W no number-pv/s, 1931) Ger-Eng
(G. Raphael -- Br&H-L 7023-pv/s) Ger-Eng
(Kalmus 2500) Ger
(GS 20285-pv/s, 1947) Ger-Eng
(Novello no number) Eng, material on rental
(H. Clough-Leighter -- ECS 1615-pv/s, 1931) Ger-Eng, choral movements only

Four movements: Duet (*sa*, 2ob, cto); Arioso (*t*, str, cto, 2ob doubling vnI); Chorus (2ob, str, cto); Chorale (2ob, str, cto, plus cornetto & 3trb doubling chorus). The cornetto and trombones merely double the choral parts in the final movement. The *sa* duet is suitable for performance by the SA choral sections.

Study scores: *BG*, vol. 5; *NAsW*, series 1, vol. 8; EE, no. 1047-m/s; Kalmus no. 811-m/s.

No. 33, *Allein zu dir, Herr Jesu Christ (Alone in Thee, Lord Jesus Christ)*, 1724, thirteenth Sunday after Trinity, 32pp, 26min.
SATB / atb / 2ob, 2vn, va, cto-org

(Br&H-W 6482-pv/s, 1968) Ger
(Br&H-W 4533) Ger-Eng, ch/s
(W. H. Bernstein -- Br&H-L 7033-pv/s) Ger-Eng, material on rental
(Kalmus 6648-pv/s) Ger, no inst/pts

Six movements: Chorus (tutti); Recitative and Arioso (*b*, cto); Aria (*a*, str, cto); Recitative (*t*, cto); Duet (*tb*, 2ob, cto); Chorale (tutti doubling chorus). The *tb* duet is suitable for performance by the TB choral sections.

Study scores: *BG*, vol. 7; *NAsW*, series 1, vol. 21; Kalmus, no. 814-m/s.

No. 36, *Schwingt freudig euch empor (Soar Joyfully on High)*, 1731, first Sunday of Advent, 36pp, 31min.
SATB / s[a]tb / 2ob d'amore, 2vn, va, cto-org

    (Alfred Dürr -- BV BA5101, 1956) Ger, ch/s
    (Br&H-W 4536) Ger-Eng, ch/s
    (Charles Sanford Terry -- Br&H-W 7036-pv/s, 1970) Ger-Eng
    (B. Todt -- Br&H-L 7036-pv/s) Ger, rent f/s & inst/pts
    (Kalmus 6536-pv/s) Ger, no inst/pts

    Eight movements in two parts: Part I: Chorus (2ob d'amore in unison, str, cto); Chorale-duet (*sa*, 2ob d'amore doubling *sa*, cto); Aria (*t*, ob d'amore solo, cto); Chorale (tutti doubling chorus). Part II: Aria (*b*, str, cto); Chorale-solo (*t*, 2ob d'amore, cto); Aria (*s*, vn solo, cto); Chorale (tutti doubling chorus). The *sa* chorale-duet and the *t* chorale-solo are suitable for performance by the SA and the T choral sections, respectively.
    Study scores: *BG*, vol. 7; *NAsW*, series 1, vol. 1; Kalmus, no. 815-m/s; BV, no. TP10-m/s.

No. 37, *Wer da glaubet und getauft wird (We Believe and Are Baptised)*, 1724, Ascension Day, 22pp, 21min.
SATB / [sa]tb / 2ob d'amore, 2vn, va, cto

    (Hans Grischkat -- HV 10.218) Ger-Eng, ch/s
    (Br&H-W 4537) Ger-Eng, ch/s
    (Roberts -- Br&H-W no number, 1937) Ger-Eng
    (Kalmus 4493) Ger
    (G. Raphael -- Br&H-L 7030-pv/s) Ger-Eng, rent f/s & inst/pts
    (Novello no number-pv/s) Ger-Eng, rent ch/s, no inst/pts

    Six movements: Chorus (tutti); Aria (*t*, cto); Chorale-duet (*sa*, cto); Recitative (*b*, str, cto); Aria (*b*, ob d'amore, str, cto); Chorale (tutti doubling chorus). The *sa* chorale-duet is suitable for performance by the SA choral sections.
    Study scores: *BG*, vol. 7; *NAsW*, series 1, vol. 12; EE, no. 1068-m/s; Kalmus, no. 815-m/s.

No. 38, *Aus tiefer Noth schrei' ich zu dir (In My Despair I Cry to Thee)*, 1724, twenty-first Sunday after Trinity, 16pp, 21 min.
SATB / sat[b] / 2ob, 4trb, 2vn, va, cto

(Br&H-W 4538) Ger-Eng, ch/s
(John E. West -- HWG GB389-pv/s) Eng, rent inst/pts
(G. Raphael -- Br&H-L 7038-pv/s) Ger-Eng, rent f/s & inst/pts
(Kalmus 5371) Eng
(John E. West -- Novello no number) Eng, material on rental
(Rev. Walter Williams -- ECS 1246-pv/s, 1938) choral movements only

Six movements; Chorus (tutti doubling chorus); Recitative (*a*, cto); Aria (*t*, 2ob, cto); Arioso (*s*, cto); Trio (*sab*, cto); Chorale (tutti doubling chorus). The trombones merely double the choral parts. The *sab* trio is suitable for performance by the SAB choral sections.
Study scores: *BG*, vol. 7; *NAsW*, series 1, vol. 25; EE, no. 1066-m/s; Kalmus, no. 816-m/s.

No. 44, *Sie werden euch in den Bann thun (Ye Shall from God's House Be Cast Forth)*, 1724, Sunday after Ascension Day, 22pp. 21min.
SATB / s[at]b / 2ob, 2vn, va, cto-bn

(Br&H-W 6550-pv/s, 1969) Ger
(E. H. Thorne and G. W. Daisley -- Br&H-W 6266-pv/s, 1932) Eng-Ger
(Br&H-W 7044-pv/s) Ger-Eng, ch/s, rent f/s & inst/pts
(Kalmus 4495) Ger
(Br&H-L 24026-pv/s, 1904) Eng
(G. Raphael --Br&H-L 7044-pv/s) Ger-Eng, rent f/s & inst/pts

Seven movements: Duet (*tb*, 2ob, cto); Chorus (2ob doubling vnI & vnII, va, cto); Aria (*a*, ob, cto); Chorale-solo (*t*, cto); Recitative (*b*, cto); Aria (*s*, 2ob doubling vnI & vnII, va, cto); Chorale (tutti doubling chorus). The bassoon doubles the continuo throughout. The violins have no separate parts; instead they consistently double the oboe lines. The *tb* duet, *t* chorale-solo, and *a* aria are suitable for performance by the TB, T, and A choral sections, respectively.
Study scores: *BG*, vol. 10; *NAsW*, series 1, vol. 12; Kalmus, no. 818-m/s.

No. 47, *Wer sich selbst erhöhet, der soll erniedriget werden (He Who Self Exalteth Shall Soon with Contempt Be Humbled)*, 1726, seventeenth Sunday after Trinity, 32pp, 25min.
SATB / sb / 2ob, 2vn, va, cto-org

(Br&H-W 4547) Ger, ch/s
(Kalmus 4496) Ger
(B. Todt -- Br&H-L 7047-pv/s) Ger, rent f/s & inst/pts

Five movements: Chorus (tutti); Aria (*s*, org obbligato, cto); Recitative (*b*, str, cto); Aria (*b*, ob, vn, cto); Chorale (tutti doubling chorus).
Study scores: *BG*, vol. 10; *NAsW*, series 1, vol. 23; Kalmus, no. 819-m/s.

No. 61, *Nun komm, der Heiden Heiland [1. Komposition] (Come, Redeemer of Our Race [1st Composition])*, 1723, first Sunday of Advent, 23pp, 20min.
SATB / stb / 2vn, 2va, cto-bn

(Günter Raphael -- BV BA5105, 1957) Ger, ch/s
(Hans Grischkat -- HV 10.025, 1966) Ger-Eng, ch/s
(Br&H-W 4561, 1970) Ger-Eng, ch/s
(Kalmus 2511) Eng
(HWG GB388-pv/s) Eng, rent inst/pts
(Ivor Atkins -- Novello 07-0005-0300-pv/s) Ger-Eng, rent inst/pts
(G. Schreck -- Br&H-L 7061-pv/s) Ger-Fr
(Br&H-L 2911) Ger, ch/pts

Six movements: Overture (Tutti); Recitative and Arioso (*t*, cto); Aria (*t*, vn & va in unison, cto); Recitative (*b*, str, cto); Aria (*s*, cto); Chorale (tutti). The bassoon merely doubles the continuo bass in the first movement and the vocal bass in the last. The *t* aria is suitable for performance by the T choral section, but the *t* Recitative and Arioso is not.
Study scores: *BG*, vol. 16; *NAsW*, series 1, vol. 1; *NBG*, Jahrgang 2-2; *DCS*, no. 26; *EGC*; EE, no. 1046-m/s; Kalmus, no. 821-m/s; BV, no. TP51-m/s.

No. 62, *Nun komm, der Heiden Heiland [2. Komposition] (Come, Redeemer of Our Race [2nd Composition])*, 1724, first Sunday of Advent, 30pp, 18min.
SATB / [*sa*]*tb* / 2ob, hn, 2vn, va, cto

(Günter Raphael -- BV BA5106, 1957) Ger, ch/s
(Hans Grischkat -- HV 10.030) Ger-Eng, ch/s
(Charles Sanford Terry -- Br&H-W 7062-pv/s, 1971) Eng-Ger
(Br&H-W 4562) Ger-Eng, ch/s
(Kalmus 2512) Ger
(B. Todt -- Br&H-L 7062-pv/s) Ger, rent f/s & inst/pts

Six movements: Chorus (tutti, hn doubling S); Aria (*t*, 2ob, str, cto); Recitative (*b*, cto); Aria (*b*, 2vn & va in unison, cto); Recitative-duet (*sa*, str, cto); Chorale (tutti doubling chorus). The horn merely doubles S in the first and last movements. The *sa* recitative-duet is suitable for performance by the SA choral sections.
Study scores: *BG*, vol. 16; *NAsW*, series 1, vol. 1; *EE*, no. 1048-m/s; Kalmus, no. 821-m/s.

No. 64, *Sehet, welch' eine Liebe hat uns der Vater erzeiget (See Now What Great Affection on Us the Father Hath Showered)*, 1723, third day of Christmas, 20pp, 27min.
SATB / *sab* / ob d'amore, cornetto(trp), 3trb, 2vn, va, cto-org

(Br&H-W 4564) Ger-Eng, ch/s
(Charles Sanford Terry -- Br&H-W 7064-pv/s, 1971) Ger-Eng
(Kalmus 4502) Ger-Eng
(E. Neumann -- Br&H-L 7064-pv/s) Ger-Eng, rent inst/pts
(Choudens 17097-pv/s, 1928) Fr
(W. G. Whittaker -- OUP 46.022-pv/s, 1925) Eng-Ger, rent inst/pts, ch/s, out of print

Eight movements: Chorus (tutti, except ob d'amore, doubling chorus); Chorale (tutti, except ob d'amore, doubling chorus); Recitative (*a*, cto); Chorale (tutti, except ob d'amore, doubling chorus); Aria (*s*, str, cto); Recitative (*b*, cto); Aria (*a*, ob d'amore, cto); Chorale (tutti, except ob d'amore, doubling chorus). The cornetto and trombones merely double the chorus parts. The *s* aria is suitable for performance by the S choral section.
Study scores: *BG*, vol. 16; *NBG*, Jahrgang 2-2; *NAsW*, series 1, vol. 3; Kalmus, no. 822m/s.

No. 72, *Alles nur nach Gottes Willen (All Things Move as God Doth Will Them)*, 1726, third Sunday of Epiphany, 28pp, 23min.
SATB / *sab* / 2ob, 2vn, va, cto

(Br&H-W 4572) Ger-Eng, ch/s
(Br&H-W 4572-pv/s, 1967) Ger
(Kalmus 4505) Ger
(G. Raphael -- Br&H-L 7072-pv/s) Ger-Eng, rent f/s & inst/pts

Five movements: Chorus (tutti); Recitative, Arioso, and Aria (*a*, 2vn, cto); Recitative (*b*, cto); Aria (*s*, obI, str, cto); Chorale (tutti doubling chorus).
Study scores: *BG*, vol. 18; *NAsW*, series 1, vol. 6; Kalmus, no. 825-m/s.

No. 73, *Herr, wie du willt, so schick's mit mir (Lord as Thou Wilt, so Deal with Me)*, 1724, third Sunday of Epiphany, 18pp, 19min.
SATB / *stb* / 2ob, [hn], 2vn, va, cto-org

(Br&H-W 4573) Ger-Eng-Fr, ch/s
(Kalmus 4506) Ger
(G. Raphael -- Br&H-L 7073-pv/s, 1935) Ger-Eng-Fr, rent f/s & inst/pts

Five movements: Chorus and Recitative (*stb*, tutti); Aria (*t*, obI, cto); Recitative (*b*, cto); Aria (*b*, str, cto); Chorale (tutti, except hn, doubling chorus). The horn has an obbligato part in the first movement, though an alternate part for organ manual is indicated.
Study scores: *BG*, vol. 18; *NAsW*, series 1, vol. 6; Kalmus, no. 825-m/s.

No. 92, *Ich hab' in Gottes Herz und Sinn (To God I Give My Heart and Soul)*, 1725, Septuagesima, 34pp, 37min.
SATB / satb / 2ob d'amore, 2vn, va, cto

(Br&H-W 7092-pv/s) Ger, ch/s, rent f/s & inst/pts
(Br&H-L 7092-pv/s) Ger, rent f/s & inst/pts
(Novello no number) Ger, material on rental
(Kalmus 6561-pv/s) Ger, no inst/pts

Nine movements: Chorus (tutti); Recitative and Chorale-solo (*b*, cto); Aria (*t*, str, cto); Chorale-solo (*a*, 2ob d'amore, cto); Recitative (*t*, cto); Aria (*b*, cto); Recitative and Chorale (*satb*, [SATB], cto); Aria (*s*, ob d'amoreI, str, cto); Chorale (tutti doubling chorus). The *a* chorale-solo is suitable for performance by the A choral section.
Study scores: *BG*, vol. 22; *NAsW*, series 1, vol. 7; *EE*, no. 1033-m/s; Kalmus, no. 830-m/s.

No. 93, *Wer nur den lieben Gott lässt walten (Whoso Will Suffer God To Guide Him)*, 1724, fifth Sunday after Trinity, 24pp, 24min.
SATB / [sa]tb / 2ob, 2vn, va, cto

(Br&H-W 4593) Ger-Eng, ch/s
(E. H. Thorne and G. W. Daisley -- Br&H-W 7093-pv/s, 1934) Ger-Eng
(G. Raphael -- Br&H-L 7093-pv/s) Ger-Eng
(Kalmus 2520) Ger
(Pointer -- Novello no number) Eng, material on rental

Seven movements: Chorus (tutti); Recitative and Chorale-solo (*b*, cto), Aria (*t*, str, cto); Duet and Instrumental Chorale (*sa*, 2vn & va in unison, cto); Recitative and Chorale-solo (*t*, cto); Aria (*s*, obI, cto); Chorale (tutti doubling chorus). The *sa* duet and *s* aria are suitable for performance by the SA and S choral sections, respectively.
Study scores: *BG*, vol. 22; *NAsW*, series 1, vol. 17; *EE*, no. 1067-m/s; Kalmus, no. 830-m/s.

No. 98, *Was Gott thut, das ist wohlgethan [2. Komposition] (What God Does, Only That Is Right [2nd Composition])*, 1726, twenty-first Sunday after Trinity, 18pp, 19min.
SATB / satb / 2ob da caccia(eh), 2vn, va, cto

(Br&H-W 4598) Ger, ch/s
(Kalmus 4513) Ger
(Br&H-L 7098-pv/s) Ger, rent f/s & inst/pts

Five movements: Chorus (2ob & ob da caccia doubling chorus, str, cto); Recitative (*t*, cto); Aria (*s*, obI solo, cto); Recitative (*a*, cto); Aria (*b*, 2vn in unison, cto). Of the three wind instruments, only the first oboe has a separate part (in the third movement), whereas the second oboe and the oboe da caccia merely double the chorus (in the first movement).

Study scores: *BG*, vol. 22; *NAsW*, series 1, vol. 25; Kalmus, no. 832-m/s.

No. 99, *Was Gott thut, das ist wohlgethan [1. Komposition] (What God Does, Only That Is Right [1st Composition])*, 1724, fifteenth Sunday after Trinity, 24pp, 23min.
SATB / [s]atb / fl, ob d'amore, hn, 2vn, va, cto

(Br&H-W 7099-pv/s) Ger, ch/s, rent f/s & inst pts
(B. Todt -- Br&H-L 7099-pv/s) Ger, rent f/s & inst/pts
(Kalmus 6567-pv/s) Ger, no inst pts

Six movements: Chorus (tutti, hn doubling S); Recitative and Arioso (*b*, cto); Aria (*t*, fl, cto); Recitative and Arioso (*a*, cto); Duet (*sa*, fl, ob d'amore, cto); Chorale (tutti doubling chorus). The horn merely doubles S in the first and last movements. The *sa* duet is suitable for performance by the SA choral sections.

Study scores: *BG*, vol. 22; *NAsW*, series 1, vol. 22; Kalmus, no. 832-m/s.

No. 106, *Gottes Zeit ist die allerbeste Zeit (God's Time Is the Best)*, 1707, funeral, 28pp, 22min.
SATB / a[t]b / 2rc(fl), 2va da gamba(vc), cto

(Paul Horn -- HV 31.106, 1977) Ger-Eng, ch/s
(BrɛH-W 4606, 1964) Ger-Eng, ch/s
(Kalmus 2525) Eng
(J. Troutbeck -- Novello 07-0009-0600-pv/s) Eng-Ger, rent inst/pts
(O. Schröder -- BrɛH-L 7106-pv/s) Ger-Eng, rent inst/pts
(BrɛH-L 2956, 1913) Ger, ch/pts
(Frank Damrosch -- GS 1056-pv/s, 1927) Eng, rent f/s ɛ inst/pts
(CF RCC-B10) Ger, no ch/s, rent inst/pts

After an opening instrumental Sonatina, several sections flow directly from one to another: Chorus (tutti); Aria (*t*, 2rc, str, cto); Aria (*b*, 2rc, cto); Chorus (tutti); Duet (*ab*, str, cto); Chorale and Chorus (tutti). The *t* aria, *b* aria, and a portion of the *a* part of the *ab* duet are suitable for performance by the T, B, and A choral sections, respectively.
Study scores: *BG*, vol. 23; *NAsW*, series 1, vol. 34; *NBG*, Jahrgang 27-1; *EGC*; EE, no. 1007-m/s; Kalmus, no. 834-m/s; BBL, no. 68-m/s; Ph, no. 106-m/s.

No. 108, *Es ist euch gut, dass ich hingehe (It Is for Your Good that I Now Leave You)*, 1725, fourth Sunday after Easter, 26pp, 20min.
SATB / atb / 2ob d'amore, 2vn, va, cto

(BrɛH-W 4608) Ger, ch/s
(Kalmus 4515) Ger
(B. Todt -- BrɛH-L 7108-pv/s) Ger, rent f/s ɛ inst/pts

Six movements: Aria (*b*, ob d'amore, str, cto); Aria (*t*, vn solo, cto); Recitative (*t*, cto); Chorus (2ob d'amore doubling 2vn, va, cto); Aria (*a*, str, cto); Chorale (tutti doubling chorus). Only one oboe d'amore has a separate part, and that in only the first movement.
Study scores: *BG*, vol. 23; *NAsW*, series 1, vol. 12; Kalmus, no. 835-m/s; BV, no. TP82-m/s.

No. 111, *Was mein Gott will, das g'scheh' allzeit (What My God Wills, That Happens Always)*, 1725, third Sunday after Epiphany, 26pp, 24min.
SATB / sa[t]b / 2ob, 2vn, va, cto

(Br&H-W 7111-pv/s) Ger, ch/s, rent f/s & inst/pts
(B. Todt -- Br&H-L 7111-pv/s) Ger, rent f/s & inst/pts
(Kalmus 6577-pv/s) Ger, no inst/pts

Six movements: Chorus (2ob, str, cto); Aria (*b*, cto); Recitative (*a*, cto); Duet (*at*, str, cto); Recitative and Arioso (*s*, 2ob, cto); Chorale (tutti doubling chorus). The *at* duet is suitable for performance by the AT choral sections.
Study scores: *BG*, vol. 24; *NAsW*, series 1, vol. 6; Kalmus, no. 836-m/s.

No. 116, *Du Friedefürst, Herr Jesu Christ (Lord Christ, Thou Art the Prince of Peace)*, 1724, twenty-fifth Sunday after Trinity, 24pp, 21min.
SATB / [s]at[b] / 2ob d'amore, hn, 2vn, va, cto

(HWG no number-pv/s) Eng, rent inst/pts
(Br&H-W 7116-pv/s) Ger-Eng, rent f/s & inst/pts
(G. Raphael -- Br&H-L 7116-pv/s) Ger-Eng, rent f/s & inst/pts
(Novello no number) Ger-Eng, material on rental
(Kalmus 6580-pv/s) Eng, no inst/pts

Six movements: Chorus (tutti, hn doubling S); Aria (*a*, ob d'amore solo, cto); Recitative (*t*, cto); Trio (*stb*, cto); Recitative (*a*, str, cto); Chorale (tutti doubling chorus). The horn merely doubles S in the first and last movements. The *stb* trio is suitable for performance by the STB choral sections.
Study scores: *BG*, vol. 24; *NAsW*, series 1, vol. 27; Kalmus, no. 837-m/s.

No. 118, *O Jesu Christ, mein's Lebens Licht [1. Instrumentierung]*
(*O Jesus Christ, My Life and Light [1st Instrumentation]*),
c. 1737, funeral, 10pp, 7min.
EBM ed :   SATB / 3trp, 2trb, 2ww+[ww]
OUP ed :   SATB / 4cornets, 2eup(brh), tba
Other eds: SATB / 2litui, 3trb, cornetto

      (Emil Kahn, arr -- EBM MC6A, 1948) Eng
      (Br&H-W 7118-pv/s, 1964) Ger-Eng, ch/s, rent f/s & inst/pts
      (Ifor Jones -- GS 1886-pv/s, 1947) Eng-Ger, rent f/s &
        inst/pts
      (G. Raphael -- Br&H-L 7118-pv/s) Ger-Eng, material on rental
      (Kalmus 6050-pv/s) Ger-Eng, no inst/pts
      (Novello no number-pv/s) Ger-Eng, rent ch/s, no inst/pts
      (Stanley Roper, arr -- OUP 42.218-pv/s, 1942) Eng-Ger, out
        of print

      This is not a cantata at all, but a one-movement chorus
in which S presents a chorale tune in long notes above
freely imitative counterpoint in ATB. The EBM and OUP
editions are efforts to provide a modern alternative scoring
for the obsolete lituus (a high pitched horn) and cornetto (a
wind instrument with finger holes and cup-shaped
mouthpiece). Bach later made a second instrumentation of the
work for winds and strings.
      Study scores: *BG*, vol. 24; *NAsW*, series 1, vol. 34;
NBG, Jahrgang 17-1 & 17-2; Kalmus, no. 838-m/s.

No. 121, *Christum wir sollen loben schon (Lord Christ We Now
Thy Praises Sing)*, 1724, second day of Christmas, 18pp,
24min.
SATB / *satb* / ob d'amore, cornetto(trp), 3trb, 2vn, va, cto

      (Br&H-W 7121-pv/s) Ger, rent f/s & inst/pts
      (B. Todt -- Br&H-L 7121-pv/s) Ger, material on rental
      (Kalmus 6583-pv/s) Ger, no inst/pts
      (W. G. Whittaker -- OUP 46.479-pv/s, 1926) Eng-Ger, rent
        inst/pts, out of print

      Six movements: Chorus (tutti doubling chorus); Aria
(*t*, ob d'amore, cto); Recitative (*a*, cto); Aria (*b*, str, cto);
Recitative (*s*, cto); Chorale (tutti doubling chorus). The
cornetto and trombones merely double the voices.
      Study scores: *BG*, vol. 26; *NAsW*, series 1, vol. 3;
Kalmus, no. 839-m/s.

No. 124, *Meinen Jesum lass' ich nicht (Never Jesus Will I Leave)*, 1725, first Sunday after Epiphany, 20pp, 19min.
SATB / [*sa*]*tb* / ob d'amore, hn, 2vn, va, cto

(Br&H-W 4624) Ger-Eng, ch/s
(G. Raphael -- Br&H-L 7124-pv/s, 1934) Ger-Eng, rent f/s & inst/pts
(Kalmus 9306-pv/s) Ger, no inst/pts

Six movements: Chorus (ob d'amore, str, cto, plus hn doubling S); Recitative (*t*, cto); Aria (*t*, ob d'amore, str, cto); Recitative (*b*, cto); Duet (*sa*, cto); Chorale (tutti doubling chorus). The horn merely doubles S in the first and last movements. The *sa* duet is suitable for performance by the SA choral sections.
Study scores: *BG*, vol. 26; *NAsW*, series 1, vol. 5; Kalmus, no. 839-m/s.

No. 131, *Aus der Tiefe rufe ich, Herr, zu dir (From the Deep, Lord, Cried I Out to Thee)*, 1708, 28pp, 27min.
SATB / [*sa*]*tb* / ob, bn, vn, 2va, cto

(Br&H-W 4631, 1975) Ger-Eng, ch/s
(Hans Grischkat -- HV 31.131, 1960) Ger-Eng, ch/s
(J. Michael Diack -- Br&H-W no number-pv/s, 1932) Ger-Eng
(Kalmus 2528) Ger
(G. Raphael -- Br&H-L 7131-pv/s) Ger-Eng, rent f/s & inst/pts
(Novello no number-pv/s) Ger-Eng, rent ch/s, no inst/pts

Five movements: Chorus (tutti); Duet (*sa*, ob, cto); Chorus (tutti); Duet (*at*, cto); Chorus (tutti). The *s* and *a* parts of the two duets are chorale tunes and thus are suitable for performance by the S and A choral sections, respectively.

No. 133, *Ich freue mich in dir (In Thee Do I Rejoice)*, 1724, third day of Christmas, 28pp, 22min.
SATB / satb / 2ob d'amore, cornetto(hn)(trp), 2vn, va, cto

(C. S. Terry -- Br&H-W 6382-pv/s, 1965) Ger-Eng
(Br&H-W 4633) Ger, ch/s
(Kalmus 4519) Ger
(Br&H-L 2983) Ger, rent inst/pts

Six movements: Chorus (str, cto, 2ob d'amore doubling vnII & va, cornetto doubling S); Aria (*a*, 2ob d'amore, cto); Recitative and Arioso (*t*, cto); Aria (*s*, str, cto); Recitative and Arioso (*b*, cto); Chorale (tutti doubling chorus). The cornetto merely doubles S in the first and last movements.
Study scores: *BG*, vol. 28; *NAsW*, series 1, vol. 3; Lea, no. 80-m/s; Kalmus, no. 841-m/s.

No. 134, *Ein Herz, das seinen Jesum lebend weiss (A Heart that Knows His Jesus Lives)*, 1724, third day of Easter, 36pp, 29min.
SATB / at / 2ob, 2vn, va, cto

(Günter Raphael -- BV BA5107, 1960) Ger
(Br&H-W 4634, 1969) Ger, ch/pts
(Br&H-L 7134-pv/s) Ger, material on rental
(Kalmus 6590-pv/s) Ger, no inst/pts

Six movements: Recitative and Arioso (*at*, cto); Aria (*t*, 2ob, str, cto); Recitative (*at*, cto); Duet (*at*, str, cto); Recitative (*at*, cto); Chorus (tutti).
Study scores: *BG*, vol. 28; *NAsW*, series 1, vol. 10; Kalmus, no. 842-m/s.

No. 135, *Ach Herr, mich armen Sünder (Oh Lord, Relent, I Pray Thee)*, 1724, third Sunday of Trinity, 16pp, 19min.
SATB / *atb* / 2ob, cornetto(hn)(trp), trb, 2vn, va, cto

(Ifor Jones -- GS 1887-pv/s, 1947) Ger-Eng, rent f/s & inst/pts
(Br&H-W 7135-pv/s) Ger, ch/s, rent f/s & inst/pts
(Br&H-L 7135-pv/s) Ger, material on rental
(H. Clough-Leighter -- ECS 1724-pv/s, 1936) Ger-Eng, choral movements only
(Kalmus 6591-pv/s) Ger, no inst/pts

Six movements: Chorus (2ob, str, cto, trb doubling B); Recitative (*t*, cto); Aria (*t*, 2ob, cto); Recitative (*a*, cto); Aria (*b*, str, cto); Chorale (tutti doubling chorus). The cornetto and trombone merely double choral parts.
Study scores: *BG*, vol. 28; *NAsW*, series 1, vol. 16; Kalmus, no. 842-m/s.

No. 138, *Warum betrübst du dich, mein Herz (And Why Cast Down Art Thou, My Heart)*, 1723, fifteenth Sunday after Trinity, 24pp, 20min.
SATB / *satb*/ 2ob d'amore, 2vn, va, cto

(Br&H-W 7138-pv/s) Ger, ch/s, rent f/s & inst/pts
(B. Todt -- Br&H-L 7138-pv/s) Ger, rent f/s & inst/pts
(Kalmus 6593-pv/s) Ger, no inst/pts

Seven movements: Chorus and Recitative (*at*, tutti); Recitative (*b*, cto); Chorus and Recitative (*sa*, tutti); Recitative (*t*, cto); Aria (*b*, str, cto); Recitative (*a*, cto); Chorale (tutti).
Study scores: *BG*, vol. 28; *NAsW*, series 1, vol. 22; Lea, no. 107-m/s; Kalmus, no. 843-m/s.

No. 139, *Wohl dem, der sich auf seinen Gott ('Tis Well with Him Who Trusts in God)*, 1724, twenty-third Sunday after Trinity, 24pp, 24min.
SATB / satb / 2ob d'amore, 2vn, va, cto

(Br&H-W 7139-pv/s) Ger, ch/s, rent f/s & inst/pts
(B. Todt -- Br&H-L 7139-pv/s) Ger, material on rental
(Kalmus 6594-pv/s) Ger, no inst/pts

    Six movements: Chorus (2ob d'amore, str, cto); Aria (*t*, 2vn in unison, cto); Recitative (*a*, cto); Aria (*b*, 2ob d'amore in unison, 2vn in unison, cto); Recitative (*s*, str, cto); Chorale (tutti doubling chorus).
    Study scores: *BG*, vol. 28; *NAsW*, series 1, vol. 26; Lea, no. 107-m/s; Kalmus, no. 843-m/s.

No. 141, *Das ist je gewisslich wahr (This a Faithful Saying Is)*, c. 1721, third Sunday of Advent, 14pp, 10min.
SATB / a[t]b / 2ob, 2vn, va, cto

(Br&H-W 7141-pv/s) Ger; ch/s; rent f/s & inst/pts
(B. Todt -- Br&H-L 7141-pv/s) Ger, rent f/s & inst/pts
(Kalmus 6595-pv/s) Ger, no inst/pts

    Four movements: Chorus (2ob, str, cto); Aria (*t*, 2ob, str, cto); Recitative (*a*, cto); Aria (*b*, str, cto). The *t* aria is suitable for performance by the T choral section.
    This cantata is included for the sake of completeness only, for it is not by J. S. Bach. Research has established that its actual composer is Georg Philipp Telemann.
    Study scores: *BG*, vol. 30; *NAsW*, series 1, vol. 41; Lea, no. 108-m/s; Kalmus, no. 843-m/s.

No. 142, *Uns ist ein Kind geboren (For Us A Child Is Born)*, c. 1713, Christmas, 24pp, 20min.
Galaxy 1939 ed: SATB / a[tb] / 2vn, va, cto
Galaxy 1940 ed: SSA / a[s] / 2vn, va, cto
ECS ed: SSAA / kbd

> (Sidney Biden, arr -- Galaxy 1.1012.2-SATB-pv/s, 1939) Eng-Ger, rent inst/pts
> (K. K. Davis & Channing Lefebvre, arr -- Galaxy 1.1841.1-SSA-pv/s, 1940) Eng-Ger, rent inst/pts
> (Arthur S. Talmadge, arr -- ECS 1608-SSAA-pv/s, 1953) Eng-Ger, choral movements only, no inst/pts

Eight movements: Sinfonia (str); Chorus (tutti); Aria (b[a], 2vn, cto); Chorus (tutti); Aria (t[s], 2vn, cto); Recitative (a, cto); Aria (a, 2vn, cto); Chorale (tutti). All the arias are suitable for performance by the respective choral sections.

These editions are arrangements of the original scoring (SATB / atb / 2fl, 2ob, 2vn, va, cto). Piano-vocal scores of the original SATB version are available from: EBM (Eng-Ger), GS (Eng-Ger), Kalmus (Ger-Eng), Br&H-W (Ger), Br&H-L (Ger), and Novello (Ger).

This cantata is included for the sake of completeness only, for it is not by J. S. Bach. Research has shown that its actual composer is most likely Johann Kuhnau.

Study scores: *BG*, vol. 30; *NBG*, Jahrgang 25-1; *NAsW*, series 1, vol. 41; Lea, no. 108-m/s; Kalmus, no. 844-m/s.

No. 144, *Nimm was dein ist, und gehe hin (Take What Is Thine and Go Thy Way)*, 1724, Septuagesima, 16pp, 16min.
SATB / s[a]t / ob d'amore, 2vn, va, cto

(BV no number) Ger, ch/s
(Br&H-W 4643) Ger, ch/s
(Kalmus 2532) Ger
(B. Todt -- Br&H-L 7144-pv/s) Ger, rent f/s & inst/pts
(OUP no number-pv/s, 1929) Eng, out of print

Six movements: Chorus (cto); Aria (*a*, str, cto); Chorale (cto); Recitative (*t*, cto); Aria (*s*, ob d'amore, cto); Chorale (SATB, cto). The *a* aria is suitable for performance by the A choral section.
Some musicologists have suggested that J. S. Bach is not the actual composer of this cantata, but this fact has not been firmly established.
Study scores: *BG*, vol. 30; *NAsW*, series 1, vol. 41; BV, no. TP56-m/s; Kalmus, no. 844-m/s.

No. 150, *Nach dir, Herr, verlanget mich (Lord, My Soul Doth Thirst for Thee)*, c. 1709, funeral, 30pp, 19min.
SATB / [satb] / 2vn, bn, cto

(Klaus Hofmann -- HV 31.150, 1977) Ger-Eng, ch/s
(Br&H-W 4650, 1964) Ger, ch/s
(Stewart Wilson -- Br&H-W no number-pv/s, 1932) Ger-Eng
(Kalmus 4521) Ger-Eng
(G. Raphael -- Br&H-L 7150-pv/s, 1960) Ger-Eng, rent f/s & inst/pts
(Novello no number) Ger-Eng, material on rental

Seven movements: Sinfonia (str, bn, cto); Chorus (tutti); Aria (*s*, 2vn in unison, cto); Chorus (tutti); Trio (*atb*, bn, cto); Chorus (tutti); Chorus (tutti). The *s* aria and the *atb* trio are suitable for performance by the S and ATB choral sections, respectively.
Study scores: *BG*, vol. 30; *NAsW*, series 1, vol. 41; *CM*; Kalmus, no. 846-m/s.

No. 161, *Komm, du süsse Todesstunde (Come Thou Lovely Hour of Dying)*, 1715, sixteenth Sunday after Trinity, 26pp, 22min.
SATB / *at* / 2rc(fl), 2vn, va, cto-org

(Br&H-W 4661) Ger-Eng, ch/s
(J. Michael Diack -- Br&H-W no number, 1930) Ger-Eng
(Bo&H no number, 1954) Eng-Ger
(BBL no number, 1943) Ger
(Kalmus 4524) Ger
(G. Raphael -- Br&H-L 7161-pv/s) Ger-Eng, rent f/s & inst/pts
(Novello no number) Ger-Eng, material on rental
(H. Clough-Leighter -- ECS 1725-pv/s, 1936) Ger-Eng, choral movements only

Six movements: Aria (*a*, 2rc, org obbligato, cto); Recitative and Arioso (*t*, cto); Aria (*t*, str, cto); Recitative and Arioso (*a*, 2rc, str, cto); Chorus (2rc, str, cto); Chorale (2rc obbligato with str & cto doubling chorus).
Study scores: *BG*, vol. 33, *NAsW*, series 1, vol. 23; EE, no. 1005-m/s; BBL, no. 6-m/s; Lea, no. 130-m/s; Kalmus, no. 848-m/s.

No. 173, *Erhöhtes Fleisch und Blut (Exhalted Flesh and Blood)*, 1731, Whit Monday, 30pp, 19min.
SATB / *sat[b]* / 2fl, 2vn, va, cto

(Br&H-W 7173-pv/s) Ger, ch/s, rent f/s & inst/pts
(Br&H-L 7173-pv/s) Ger, material on rental
(Kalmus 6615-pv/s) Ger, no inst/pts

Six movements: Recitative (*t*, str, cto); Aria (*t*, 2fl doubling vnI, str, cto); Aria (*a*, str, cto); Duet (*sb*, 2fl, str, cto); Recitative-duet (*st*, cto); Chorus (2fl, str, cto). The *sb* duet is suitable for performance by the SB choral sections.
Study scores: *BG*, vol. 35; *NAsW*, series 1, vol. 14; Kalmus, no. 851-m/s.

No. 179, *Siehe zu, dass deine Gottesfurcht nicht Heuchelei sei (Trust the Lord, Come Thou to Him)*, 1723, eleventh Sunday after Trinity, 18pp, 17min.
SATB / [s]*tb* / 2ob da caccia(eh)[doubling on 2ob], 2vn, va, cto

    (Br&H-W 7179-pv/s, 1969) Ger, ch/s, rent f/s & inst/pts
    (B. Todt -- Br&H-L 7179-pv/s) Ger, material on rental
    (Kalmus 6621-pv/s) Ger, no inst/pts

      Six movements: Chorus (str doubling chorus, cto); Recitative (*t*, cto); Aria (*t*, str, 2ob doubling vnI, cto); Recitative (*b*, cto); Aria (*s*, 2ob da caccia, cto); Chorale (tutti, except 2ob da caccia, doubling chorus). The oboes have no separate parts. The *s* aria is suitable for performance by the S choral section.
      Study score: *BG*, vol. 35; *NAsW*, series 1, vol. 20; EE, no. 1075-m/s; Kalmus, no. 852-m/s.

No. 182, *Himmelskönig, sei willkommen (King of Heaven Ever Welcome)*, 1724, Palm Sunday, 36pp, 30min.
SATB / *atb* / rc(fl), vn, 2va, vc, cto

    (Br&H-W 1195-pv/s, 1962) Ger
    (Br&H-W 4682, 1975) Ger-Fr, ch/s
    (BBL no number, 1943) Ger
    (Kalmus 2543) Ger-Fr
    (B. Todt -- Br&H-L 7182-pv/s) Ger-Fr, rent f/s & inst/pts
    (Novello no number) Ger-Fr, material on rental
    (H. Clough-Leighter -- ECS 1196-pv/s, 1931) Eng-Ger, choral movements only

      Eight movements: Sonata (rc, vn solo, 2va, cto); chorus (rc, str, cto); Recitative and Arioso (*b*, cto); Aria (*b*, vn, 2va, cto); Aria (*a*, rc, cto); Aria (*t*, cto); Chorus (tutti doubling chorus); Chorus (rc, str, cto).
      Study scores: *BG*, vol. 37; *NAsW*, series 1, vol. 8; EE, no. 1024-m/s; BBL, no. 24-m/s; Kalmus, no. 853-m/s.

No. 187, *Es wartet Alles auf dich (Dwell Not Upon the Morrow)*, 1726, seventh Sunday after Trinity, 36pp, 25min. SATB / sa[b] / 2ob, 2vn, va, cto

(Alfred Dürr -- BV no number) Ger, ch/s
(Br&H-W 4687) Ger, ch/pts
(Br&H-L 7187-pv/s) Ger, rent f/s & inst/pts
(Kalmus 6628-pv/s) Ger, no inst/pts

    Seven movements in two parts: Part I: Chorus (tutti); Recitative (*b*, cto); Aria (*a*, str, obI doubling vnI, cto). Part II: Aria (*b*, 2vn in unison, cto); Aria (*s*, ob, cto); Recitative (*s*, str, cto); Chorale (tutti doubling chorus). The *b* aria is suitable for performance by the B choral section.
    Study scores: *BG*, vol. 37; *NAsW*, series 1, vol. 18; Kalmus, no. 854-m/s.

No. 196, *Der Herr denket an uns (The Lord Remembers Us)*, 1708, wedding, 20pp, 17min. SATB / s[tb] / 2vn, va, vc, cto-org

(Br&H-W 4696, 1968) Ger, ch/s
(Kalmus 4530) Ger
(B. Todt -- Br&H-L 7196-pv/s) Ger, rent f/s & inst/pts
(Novello no number-pv/s) Ger, rent ch/s, no inst/pts

    Five movements: Sinfonia (str, cto); Chorus (tutti); Aria (*s*, 2vn in unison, cto); Duet (*tb*, str, cto); Chorus (tutti). The *tb* duet is suitable for performance by the TB choral sections.
    Study scores: *BG*, vol. 13; *NAsW*, series 1, vol. 40; Kalmus, no. 858-m/s.

PART 4 / APPENDICES

APPENDIX I

The Selected Cantatas Alphabetically by Title

The *BG* numbers of the selected cantatas are given below after each cantata's German title. These numbers may be used to easily locate the cantatas in the catalog, since the cantatas are entered in numerical order both in the catalog itself and on the contents page.

Ach Gott, vom Himmel sieh darein (2)

Ach Gott, wie manches Herzeleid [1. Komposition] (3)

Ach Herr, mich armen Sünder (135)

Allein zu dir, Herr Jesu Christ (33)

Allen nur nach Gottes Willen (72)

Aus der Tiefe rufe ich, Herr, zu dir (131)

Aus tiefer Noth schrei' ich zu dir (38)

Christ lag in Todesbanden (4)

Christ unser Herr zum Jordan kam (7)

Christum wir sollen loben schon (121)

Das ist je gewisslich wahr (141)

Der Herr denket an uns (196)

Du Friedefürst, Herr Jesu Christ (116)

Du wahrer Gott und Davids Sohn (23)

Ein Herz, das seinen Jesum lebend weiss (134)

Erhohtes Fleisch und Blut (173)

Es ist das Heil uns Kommen her (9)

Es ist euch gut, dass ich hingehe (108)

Es wartet Alles auf dich (187)

Gottes Zeit ist die allerbeste Zeit (106)

Herr, wie du willt, so schick's mit mir (73)

Himmelskönig, sei willkommen (182)

Ich freue mich in dir (133)

Ich hab' in Gottes Herz und Sinn (92)

Jesus nahm zu sich die Zwölfe (22)

APPENDIX II

The Selected Cantatas by Solo Voice Requirements

Listed below are the *BG* numbers of the selected cantatas that are performable by various individual soloists and combinations of soloists. These numbers may be used as in the previous appendix.

no soloists: 4, 118, 150

s only: 4, 150, 196

a only: 4, 150, 142

t only: 4, 23, 150

b only: 4, 150

sa: 4, 142, 150, 187

st: 4, 23, 144, 150, 196

sb: 4, 44, 47, 150, 196

at: 4, 23, 116, 134, 142, 150, 161

ab: 4, 106, 141, 142, 150

tb: 4, 9, 37, 62, 93, 124, 131, 150, 179

sat: 4, 23, 38, 116, 144, 150, 173

sab: 4, 44, 64, 72, 111, 150, 187

stb: 4, 9, 10, 36, 37, 44, 61, 62, 73, 93, 124, 131, 150, 179, 196

atb: 2, 4, 7, 9, 22, 33, 37, 62, 93, 99, 106, 108, 116, 124, 131, 135, 141, 142, 150, 182

satb: 3, 4, 9, 10, 17, 36, 37, 38, 44, 62, 92, 93, 98, 99, 111, 116, 121, 124, 131, 133, 138, 139, 150, 173

APPENDIX III

The Selected Cantatas by Occasional Appropriateness

The *BG* numbers of the selected cantatas are grouped here by the occasion for which each cantata was originally written. The specific days within the broad categories (e.g., Trinity, Christmas) for which the cantatas were written are included as a part of each cantata's entry in the catalog. Each entry may be easily located, for the cantatas are cataloged and entered on the contents page in numerical order.

Advent: 36, 61, 62, 141

Christmas: 64, 121, 133, 142

Epiphany: 3, 72, 73, 111, 124

Septuagesima: 92, 144

Quinquagesima: 22, 23

Palm Sunday: 182

Easter: 4, 108, 134

Ascension: 37, 44

Whit Monday: 173

Trinity: 2, 9, 17, 33, 38, 47, 93, 98, 99, 116, 135, 138, 139, 161, 179, 187

St. John's Day: 7

Visitation of the Blessed Virgin Mary: 10

Wedding: 196

Funeral: 106, 118, 150

ABOUT THE AUTHOR

Dr. William J. Bullock is a choral conductor of wide experience, having conducted much of the standard and more recent oratorio literature and prepared choruses for performances with professional orchestras and opera companies. He has served as choral adjudicator and guest conductor in eight states, published selected musical editions and articles, received performance and research grants from national and state agencies, and conducted concert tours of Europe. Before assuming his current position of Director of Choral Activities at Columbus College (Georgia), Dr. Bullock held the same position at the University of Southern Mississippi. He is also Director of the Columbus Civic Chorale, Inc., founder of the Six Flags Over Texas Choral Festival, a Past President of the Texas Junior College Teachers Association and of the Mississippi chapter of the American Choral Directors Association, and a biographee in several publications, including the *International Who's Who in Music*.